The Rich Man

A first-person account from hell

Reports from the next life
From Luke 16:19-21

James Olah

August 28, 2021

Jesus said: "The time came when the beggar died, and the angels carried him to Abraham's side. The rich man also died and was buried. In Hades, where he was in torment.... (He said) 'I am in agony in this fire.'"

Luke 16 22:-23

The Rich Man

A first-person account from hell
The Rich Man and Lazarus from Luke 16:19-31

James Olah

Copyright August 28, 2021
12-22-22
ISBN: 9798466439144

Address the author at jolah1968@gmail.com for permission to quote.

Cover photo courtesy http://pixabay.com

Independently Published

OLAH Books

Contents

"What good is it for someone to gain the whole world, yet forfeit their soul? Or what can anyone give in exchange for their soul?"
(Mark 8:36–37, NIV)

1. Why this book?

HELL IS A TOPIC that demands our attention, for it is not a place of comfort but of unending torment. The Bible's depiction of hell is not to be taken lightly. I use the word hell in this book because that is how most identify this place. Hell is translated from the Greek word hades.

Some think hell is contrived to scare people into church or get right with God. If you believe that, then you miss the importance of it. Hell is a topic that God warned us about as He walked this earth for 33 years. Jesus talked more about hell, hades, and the lake of fire than any other writer in the Bible. For every word Jesus spoke about heaven, he used three words warning people to avoid hell. He doesn't want us to go there. He seeks to rescue us from our rebellious decision to live on our terms.

Jesus gave us this account of hell, the book's focus, to make His teaching attention-grabbing and unforgettable. His parables or stories are far easier to remember and share with others than just presenting facts or warnings. I trust that the method by which I present The Rich Man will hold your attention as it offers significant teachings about a place most people find abhorrent to consider. This fiction story seeks to pull together biblical truth to help give you a deeper understanding of the topic.

As you read the account of the Rich Man and Lazarus in Luke 16, notice that Jesus uses a proper name. His use of a name may sound incidental, but it becomes more significant when you recognize that He does not use a specific name in any parable. With this inclusion of a proper name, many scholars believe this is not a parable but an actual account. If it is a parable, it does not change the teaching about hell.

Jesus wanted us to know some essential truths about hell because He knew people would distort the teachings of this place. The Old

Testament offers mostly shadowy pictures of the afterlife. Jesus' teachings are more specific about the afterlife, warning us not to enter our afterlife as God's enemy. He wanted us to have a realistic picture of the consequences of rejecting God. We can't ignore God, think He will overlook our sins, and welcome everyone into heaven. People avoid thinking that they are sinful enough to be eternally separated from God.

There is much sound biblical teaching about hell. My purpose is to give you a different perspective to help you better understand how these teachings clarify the kind of suffering in hell. I am inviting the Rich Man to share some of his experiences with you since his arrival there. I seek to portray his suffering through the biblical words used in the Luke 16 text and other biblical teachings, which I footnote. This story is not chronological but skips back and forth in time. Also, during my writing, I did research about near-death experiences (NDE) of heaven and hell to understand the details of life on the other side. How the Rich Man suffers in hell is my interpretation of the kind of suffering that would express the teachings found in the Bible.

I write this book not to scare people but to give them a clearer understanding of hell's reality. Ignoring hell doesn't make it go away. I hope this book challenges your thinking and gives you a more realistic insight into a place you will want to avoid. Just remember, escape is possible only before death. At the end of this book, I present an exit plan that I hope you will find helpful. I continue with the story method to explain God's provision to escape the final judgment.

Now, let's meet the Rich Man. His story is not just a narrative but a profound insight into the reality of hell. He's been anticipating your arrival so he can share details about his life. He always liked talking about himself, so you will find his story intriguing.

2. The Rich Man

YOU ARE ALL GOING TO DIE! I hope it is not today for you. However, that eventful day will reach out and grasp you, and you need to be ready. It is a serious thing to die because that seals your fate for eternity. Your decision about your faith is of utmost importance, as it determines your eternal destiny. I hope you have made or will make the right decision because death ends your opportunity to affect your eternity. Excuse me; I am getting ahead of myself. You don't even know who I am, and I'm talking to you about this issue most want to avoid. Let me introduce myself.

Hello, my name is Jokim. I am one of six sons of Jethro of Bethany. We lived outside of the great city of Jerusalem. You may have heard of my neighbor Lazarus and his two sisters, Mary and Martha. My father was a shrewd businessman who taught us the art and pleasure of making money well. My brothers and I were very close. Yes, we had our disagreements along the way, for we all had strong egos and were very competitive. You would notice that one thing consumed us all: the drive to make money. Like many Jews taken to Babylon 600 years ago, we turned from the idols of the nations around us that we worshipped and gave our devotion to another god. It was the god of wealth and shrewd business dealings. We always competed to see who could get the best deals and make the most money. That was a constant motivation in our lives. Together, we would devise business plans for making lots of money, and then, as we sat around on a cold or rainy day, we dreamed and talked about how we would spend our wealth and the honor we would receive from friends and fellow businessmen. We spoke of banquets, celebrations, and the women that would seek us out. Being rich would make the finer things of life available to us without limit. Those were our dreams, and together, we all anticipated becoming rich men as we worked together on business ventures.

The Rich Man

Some, well, many of our dealings were not done in the most honorable way. But that's the way business is done in the world. You can't be thinking of other people if you want to make money. It's a dog-eat-dog world, and we fought to become the leaders of the pack. I must tell you that using that business philosophy gave us more than satisfying results. We all became very wealthy and loved our extravagant homes and lavish living. Hosting elegant parties and having influential guests became commonplace, and of course, there were those long nights with the lovely ladies, if you know what I mean. There were always reasons to celebrate when you have lots of money, and we made many important business deals at these parties. We withheld no good thing from ourselves in our celebrations, for we always enjoyed the best of everything. We were the top dogs!

You may think you have never heard of me, but you have. I am the main character Jesus spoke of in one of his teachings. You know the other person in his story by name, but he withheld my identification. You would know me better as the rich man. Ah-ha, now the pieces of my story start to fit into place. The man associated with my story is a disgustingly poor and wretched man named Lazarus. I wonder why Jesus made him the good guy in this account. He didn't accomplish anything significant as I did.

You have heard the account of my misfortune many times. Perhaps it makes you cringe, as it should, or maybe you sweep it under your Persian rug and choose not to think of what is happening to me. If you fall into the latter description of how people respond to this teaching, you will join my company. Perhaps we will meet up one day and commiserate over our regrets and the unfairness of this constant torture.

If you think I am evil, you are not seeing me through my eyes. Sure, I made some shady dealings in my business practices, but that is how we got along. Besides, I'm not the only one, for that was a common practice with our generation, just as it is for many of you today. Despite my shrewd business dealings, I want you to know I was a good religious person. I went to the temple somewhat regularly. I tithed as a good Jew should, and I attended the feasts and celebrations at the temple. We participated in these events as regularly as the passing of time in a sand clock. We lived close to Jerusalem, and attending these feasts and celebrations didn't take much effort. I don't think we would have taken the time to participate if we lived around Galilee. After all, you have to make money while the sun shines.

Even though I was religious, it was mainly an outward show, for, at the root of all I did, it was to glorify myself and show my goodness or how religious I was. My religion was an outward show with actions and no heart, you know, like many of you who are reading this story, are living your faith. You attend synagogue or church and leave unchanged as you continue to live like the rest of the world around you, just as I did. That was also true of the religious leaders. As pious as they presented themselves, they were no different from me. We all knew how to put on a good show, but true, life-changing faith does not characterize how we expressed our faith, as small as it was. And you, my reader friend, may have accepted this type of teaching. You fear that the kind of faith God wants you to have would require more change than you are willing to agree upon. You never cared for the peer pressure to live a holy life because you enjoyed life's pleasures. So, you see, you may not be much different from me if you are judging me in your mind.

I had many opportunities to demonstrate the faith life God called us to live, but I was so taken up with myself that Lazarus was not my concern. He ought to have taken care of himself. Such people are such a drain on society. They think that because I have money, I should support them. In reality, that guy was more of an eyesore and a distraction to the beauty of my estate. All my well-dressed friends, business associates, and family came to my place for dinners and special occasions. There, greeting them, was this sorry excuse of a man who was unkempt, smelly, dirty, and full of sores. He was always asking for food or a little money. My dogs had more pity on him than I did, for they were drawn to him and licked his running sores. Why couldn't his friends take him to another place? But NOOOO, he always ended up at my gate. I think such people are useless and are a blemish to society. Face it; such people amount to nothing. He was not fit to even serve as one of my servants. Worthless!

As I think back on how I viewed Lazarus, not much has changed in my thinking since I came to this place of torment. I've had much time to reflect on my life. Sometimes, I may have been too hard on him. Then, the reality of his presence at my gate caused me to view him with disdain for spoiling the atmosphere of my formal banquets. I try to forget him, but because all I have here is time, I can't let my contempt for him go for very long. My thoughts can be compared to a dog going after a meaty bone, and I can't stop thinking about him. These constant thoughts cause me to loathe him more and more.

Jesus told the story about Lazarus and me; his explanations were short. I am the featured person in that account, and I want to fill in the gaps in my story to give you a better picture of what happened to me. Some of you may wince at the thought of learning about the place of eternal torment. Ignoring my story will not change the outcome of your eternity, as I have been reminded of that fact every day. Facing this fear of hell head-on can help you make decisions that can change your life, relationship with God, and eternity. But, if you have apathy toward God as I did, then it will soon pass, and you will obliviously proceed to death and eternity as I have. As I recount my story, remember that you must avoid the reservation desk if you want to join me here.

3. The Rich Man and Lazarus

IF YOU ARE NOT FAMILIAR with this story, why don't you take a minute and listen to what Jesus said about Lazarus and me?

19 "There was a rich man who was dressed in purple and fine linen and lived in luxury every day. 20 At his gate was laid a beggar named Lazarus, covered with sores 21 and longing to eat what fell from the rich man's table. Even the dogs came and licked his sores.

22 "The time came when the beggar died, and the angels carried him to Abraham's side. The rich man also died and was buried. 23 In Hades, where he was in torment, he looked up and saw Abraham far away, with Lazarus by his side. 24 So he called to him, 'Father Abraham, have pity on me and send Lazarus to dip the tip of his finger in water and cool my tongue because I am in agony in this fire.'

25 "But Abraham replied, 'Son, remember that in your lifetime you received your good things, while Lazarus received bad things, but now he is comforted here, and you are in agony. 26 And besides all this, between us and you, a great chasm has been set in place, so that those who want to go from here to you cannot, nor can anyone cross over from there to us.'

27 "He answered, 'Then I beg you, father, send Lazarus to my family, 28 for I have five brothers. Let him warn them so that they will not also come to this place of torment.'

29 "Abraham replied, 'They have Moses and the Prophets; let them listen to them.'

30 " 'No, father Abraham,' he said, 'but if someone from the dead goes to them, they will repent.'

31 "He said to him, 'If they do not listen to Moses and the Prophets, they will not be convinced even if someone rises from the dead.'" Luke 16:19-31 - NIV

The Rich Man

Well, there you have the account that Jesus gave of my death and the misery I face. I am here not only because of my mistreatment of Lazarus but, more specifically, of ignoring God and refusing to take Him seriously. I want to fill in the blank spaces in my story to help you better identify with me and what to expect if you choose to become my neighbor. I always enjoyed talking about myself before, which hasn't changed since I arrived here. If you are smart, you will choose the **'OTHER'** place. I hear reports that Paradise is much happier than this place. The neighborhoods are not so good here. There's plenty of riff-raff all around me. But I keep my arrogance in place, thinking I am still better than others. You caught me on a good day to explain my situation. I'm angry and foul-mouthed for many days because of my pain and disdain for God's judgment. You might have to excuse some of my language along the way. So, if you can stomach what I say, I'll let you tag long at the back of this crowd.

4.   Life was Good (Verse 19)

AS I RECALL, I thought of my existence back then. I loved living a full and exciting life. It was the fulfillment of my imaginings. People dream of having as much money as I have. They view life as I did. Life is so much better, tranquil, and filled with pleasures when you have more than enough money. I was having the time of my life, and people looked up to me. The people of my community respected me for my wealth and power and honored my presence. All the young businessmen admired me and asked for my secrets for success. I was one of those fun-loving people they wanted to have at their feasts and celebrations. The excitement I added to a party made people want to be present when they knew I would attend. When I came to an event, I had the finest clothes. My tailor was Keros from the prestigious Coconut Republic Designers, who always found the finest material and made it look fashionable. I was the envy of the town. No one, except our family, could afford this talented designer.

Those were such good days. I had it made. There was no thought of needing further preparation for the future because I had everything covered. Life would continue to be good for me, for I could feel it in my bones. Jesus knew me well and how valuable I thought I was because of my wealth and lavish living. He chose me as an example because all the wealthy Pharisees knew and admired me. He showed them that wealth didn't make a person right with God or any better than anyone else. Wealth made me and the religious leaders shortsighted because it blinded our eyes to our duty, our relationship with God, and the importance of eternity. Sometimes, I noticed those people who had genuine faith, and for a moment, I admired them, but soon, the thought of wealth wooed me back to reality. I had no reason to believe in God, for certainly, He can't provide for me any better than this. What's the use in changing my lifestyle?

"*You make known to me the path of life; you will fill me with joy in your presence, with eternal pleasures at your right hand.*"
(Psalm 16:11)

5. Life was Not so Good (Verse 20-21)

My story is very different from Lazarus's. I always viewed him as a real loser. Come on, isn't that what you think about down and outers? This guy had nothing. I imagine his parents were glad to get him out of their house every day and bestow a little misery on my life. I told them different times not to do that, but it didn't stop them from leaving him at my gate most days. Sometimes, I would leave by the back entrance to avoid him. "Why, God, does he come to my front gate every day?" That's about as serious as my prayers got with God.

This man was a drain on society and had nothing going for himself. He had no way to make money except by begging. I wonder how he hung on for so long with the diseases and sickness he had. But that smelly, dirty cripple always returned, no matter how bad things got for him. Some days, Lazarus was coughing and hacking incessantly, and he looked so sick that I wondered if he would return the next day. To my chagrin, that pathetic excuse for a man was back spoiling the beauty of my gate the following day.

Why did I not help this man? The answer is simple. I did not want other worthless people to join him because they would see me as a soft touch. Also, if I fed him or paid a doctor to take care of him, he might live longer and continue to be an annoyance to me, and he might also consider me his friend. I don't need that kind of person associated with me.

That is how I viewed him. What irritated me about him was that he always had a good attitude. Despite his pain and hopelessness, he always spoke kindly to people. He didn't seem to feel sorry for himself. How could he be so poor, sick, and miserable and still be happy? His attitude baffled me. It takes material things, money, and opportunities to indulge the flesh with wine and women to make one happy! There was something about this man that irritated me and also made me admire him. But I refused to respect him because that would rip a hole in my philosophy of life. It takes money and things to make one happy. So, I chose to despise him and do nothing to encourage him in his condition.

I told my servants never to offer him any of MY leftover food, but I don't think they always listen to me. Beggars are like dogs; if you give them food, they'll be back for more, and I wanted to do what I could to keep him away. So when I discovered one of my servants gave him food, I fired her on the spot. Making an example of someone who defied me taught a lesson to the rest of my servants. That was my food to do with as I pleased, and my servants were to serve me by doing all I commanded.

He didn't understand that I didn't want him outside my gate, so my contempt for him grew. I continued to look for ways to humiliate him through sarcasm or making fun of him and his crippled condition. I would curse him and do anything I could to make him feel uncomfortable and worthless so he wouldn't return to my gate. But he always returned and often had a smile on his face as he welcomed me. I know that smile was born out of a sarcastic motivation. As much as I thought my hatred of him was justified, I would discover that this attitude would become a source of my torment here.

6. Then We Died (Verse 22)

I DIDN'T THINK ABOUT DEATH MUCH. The thought of an afterlife was merely clutter in my mind that distracted me from the pleasures of life. I'm not going to deal with that part of my life. God can deal with me when I get there. I kept thinking there had to be some good in me because God blessed me with all my riches. I also gave a lot of money to the temple. That should mean something when I stand before God. Besides, I can't spend all my time dwelling on the afterlife because I want to live now.

Then, one day, I noticed that Lazarus was not there, and that caused me to smile. Good riddance, I said. Even though I thought his absence was only temporary, in the back of my mind, I knew he would be back in a day or two to torment me and cause me distress. But a week went by, and then two. I thought, "Am I free from this man?" as I passed through my gate the following days. Then I started to wonder where he was. So I asked my servant, Ezra, "What happened to Lazarus?" His response stunned me, "He died three weeks ago. His health further diminished, and then one morning, he didn't wake up. Do you remember that large procession a few weeks ago? That was his funeral. The townspeople liked him."

I remember thinking, 'How could a man who didn't get around impact so many people?' But as I thought about him outside of my gate, I remember people stopping often, and it seemed like they were carrying on conversations with him, and I frequently heard laughing before they left. How come that never made an impact on me until now? My self-centeredness blinded my eyes to his good qualities. After that conversation with Ezra, I often wondered why I never talked with Lazarus. But then it came to me; being around Lazarus and smelling his stench made me feel dirty and uncomfortable. When I thought of him, my skin would crawl.

Jesus told what happened when he died. The time came for him to die, and angels came to carry him to heaven. He was honored by the angels. I have since talked with the lead angel, Asriel, and he said, "Lazarus was so much fun to take to Paradise to join with Abraham. Lazarus loved the new freedom to talk, and he no longer experienced pain, and he loved being able to jump, walk, and dance. For most of his life, those were things Lazarus couldn't do. What a grand time he had when he arrived. You should have seen all the people rejoicing when they saw him come. You know friends anticipate their friends coming. He sure had a lot of them. It was one of those exceptional transports of a person to paradise."

Something about the death of Lazarus caused me to start contemplating the end of my life a little more seriously. I didn't think about it all the time, but it came into my thinking more frequently, but I brushed the thought aside each time. After all, I was a good Jew. I went to festivals and synagogues more than most of my friends, and I tithed because I wanted God's blessing on my next deal. Indeed, that would give me standing before God. Then I would think of my wealth and reasoned that God would not have honored me with so much wealth if He didn't accept me. All my wealth undoubtedly indicated God's blessing in my life. I always had an answer to detour my questions from the truth, but it never satisfied my soul. Then I thought, I'm no different from anyone else, for everyone wrestles with such thoughts. For a moment, I would think, "I wonder if I'm ready for eternity. Will God reject me? Certainly, He won't, will He?" I never avoided the fine details in business dealings, but somehow, I could table these thoughts about death before I came under too much conviction about this distant issue of life.

A year or two after Lazarus' death, my health started to decline. I didn't have as much energy as before. I rationalized that I was getting older and I was slowing down. Perhaps I was indulging a little too much at our banquets. But I knew it was more than that because it took me longer to walk up those hills on my travels. Sometimes, that extra exertion caused my chest to tighten. I was experiencing shortness of breath and sweating more than usual. But just like avoiding thinking about eternity, I avoided thinking about my health. My wife said I should see the doctor, but I was too busy, and everyone counted on me to be at work every day. I couldn't let up because there was a weekly payroll to meet.

My discomfort continued and increased until one evening. My pain became so severe it woke me out of deep sleep and increased in intensity. I woke my wife to tell her about my distress and labored breathing, and before I could say anything, I fell back on my bed, and everything went black.

A strange sensation came over me as my breathing ceased, and before I knew it, I was looking down at what was my body. The pain was gone, and I felt better than I had in years. I looked again at what I recognized as my body, and my wife was crying. She called a servant to get a doctor. I tried to tell her I was all right, but she couldn't hear me. The more I tried to communicate with her, the more frustrated I became. I tried to gather my wits about what was happening.

Abruptly I was surrounded by total blackness. At first, I was alone, and then some beings came alongside me, and something about them terrified me. **"Get away from me,"** I shouted at them. They kept coming closer, and then it felt like they were hitting me. Some even bit me. I was more confused and becoming even more terrified.

Then, quite unexpectedly, I was in a place of light. It was like a light I'd never seen before, different from the light of the sun. This light was a being, and like a candle being lit, it hit me that I was with God. I was standing in his presence. It seemed like a long time, but maybe it was only a minute or two.

He asked me in a very caring tone, "What have you done with your life?" I stammered a bit, searching for words or a defense for how I lived life. Then he said, "You have worshiped idols and wasted your opportunities to live for me. You worshiped money, pleasure, and status among friends more than you desired to honor me.

God did not make empty accusations against me. All He said was true. He then verified what He told me by causing my life to pass before my eyes. I was able to see all that I did. He showed me the good things I did and how it helped some people. But my motives nullified many of my actions. In all my good deeds, He revealed my intentions, attitudes, and all those underlying motivations that caused me to exalt myself above God and take advantage of others. He also caused me to see how I treated people, took advantage of them, or scorned them and how my actions affected their lives.

Even though things didn't look good for me, I couldn't help but notice that God wasn't angry. He was sad for me. I experienced God's love for me and His commitment to justice at that moment. It was just a brief glimpse of Him and His character, but it made me want to be with Him forever. How could I have neglected my relationship with such a wonderful, loving God? I now understood how wonderful heaven must be to dwell in His presence for eternity.

"God, I don't want to leave your presence. Let me stay here, please! I'll make it up to you. I want to get to know you and experience you in every way. I chose wrong; please, have mercy."

He allowed me to speak my mind, and when I finished, he said with a firm voice, as a judge sentencing someone. "You rejected me in life; you rejected my Son as your savior; you scoffed at my words; you placed yourself above me and worshiped the idols of gold, pleasure, and status in the way you lived. You gave yourself to wickedness rather than righteousness. You satisfied your soul with religion rather than a relationship with me." Then with sadness in his eyes, He said, "Depart from me, you who are cursed; I never knew you. Enter the eternal fire and darkness prepared for the devil and his angels."

Before I knew it, I was speeding down an enormous dark tunnel, which didn't end for several hours. Then, another fear gripped me when I wondered what would happen when I hit bottom. I would pass someone occasionally, and others seemed to fly by me on my descent.

I crash-landed in this place, and it didn't do me any physical damage, but it sure did hurt. I learned that this place is called hades, or some call it hell. Hades is a vast place with billions of people and spirit beings, which I joined. It is neither delightful nor sunny with blue skies but dark and covered with dreary clouds.

I don't know how long it took me to come to my senses when I arrived, but slowly, I became aware of my new surroundings. It is an eerie place. The beings around me were like something out of my worst nightmare. They weren't kind or respectful like most people who surrounded me in my business. They cursed me as they pushed me along and said something about taking me to my new home.

"What are they talking about?" I thought. "I like my old home and don't want a new one. I've got a perfectly good home. Why are you taking me someplace else? I don't want to go with you. **Leave me alone!** I don't recognize anyone around me. I want to be with my friends. This place is too frightening! Stop! **STOP THIS RIGHT NOW!**"

Confused and distressed, these beings offered me no explanation or comfort. There was no small talk, and no one offered any compassion. I wanted them to show me kindness or compassion during this time, for it was all new. Then, I heard something completely astounding. One of the beings said, "In the place, you will never experience any kindness or compassion again." That floored me. I couldn't believe it. Then it hit me like a ton of coconuts, "I'm really headed for Hades." My world utterly shattered before me like an egg tossed against the temple wall. All the order I established in my life, personal pleasures, wealth, and friendships will never again be an enjoyable part of my existence.

I always avoided thinking about the afterlife and certainly didn't consider that I could end up in Hades, but here I am. Now what? I'm sure I will learn all too soon what a terrible decision I made by being so self-focused and using excuses not to prioritize a relationship with God in my life. I knew I was covering up my lack of devotion to God for the sake of enjoying worldly pleasures. Now, I'm sure I will never experience any of those pleasures again.

Jokim didn't realize just how true an observation he had made.

7.   In Torment (Verse 23)

WELL, HELLO AGAIN. It's been a while since I've seen you. You were the one who followed me after I died in my mansion. I'm confident the trip to Hades scared you, as it did me. You sure made a hasty retreat when you saw where I ended up. Perhaps you thought it was a bit too real. But I see you're back. I imagine you are wondering what I have been experiencing. I'm glad you are curious because Jesus wanted my experience to help you think more realistically as you contemplate your eternity. I avoided the topic of the afterlife before I died, and I wonder if you are avoiding it as I did. Grab a jagged rock and sit down, and I'll tell you about my experiences.

On earth, you have people you care about and others you don't want to take the time to get to know; for me, it was Lazarus, and I treated him with constant contempt. Here in Hades, no one expresses love or concern about anyone. Most treat me as an enemy, others as untouchable or unclean. No one has restraint over the evil in their hearts. I live in a very unfriendly place; everyone is filled with bitterness, contempt, and suspicion. They communicate, but the language is often fouler than anything I heard on earth. There is little to no compassion expressed toward anyone. When I listen to people speak about being in this place, I have never heard anyone express regret for not submitting to God or accepting the salvation Jesus provided. They all continue to be antagonistic toward God and curse Him for relegating them to this place. Hell reveals the disdain they harbored in their heart for God and their continuous unwillingness to submit to His will. [1] We are all here because we chose to reject God in favor of living on our terms.

---

[1] They did not want to repent of their rebellious nature and submit to God.

When I arrived, constant depression and sadness filled my entire being. The unrelenting sounds of agonizing mourning were beyond anything I have ever heard in all my years on earth. For what seemed like months, a heavy cloud of extreme depression crushed my spirit. All I could think about was that I could never leave this dreadful, monotonous place or torment.

Absolute terror filled the atmosphere here; it was like a winter blizzard blowing chills down my spine. Sometimes, I recognized the beings causing the terror. Still, other times, the anxiety was just a result of the eeriness of this place's atmosphere.

The pain is beyond description. It was the kind of sharp pain that shoots through your whole being, and you scream for relief, but no respite comes. The pain is not in any particular place but radiates through every part of my body. Also, my thoughts cause pain because of regret, shame, guilt, and a sense of total loss of all that is good.

There are words and phrases that I can use to describe the horror of my home or neighborhood. This is a place of torment, where we are all miserable, and as I said a moment ago, a depressing place. Sunshine and happy times filled my life on earth, but intense darkness, screaming, and foul odors are my daily routine here. Those who were very evil, such as rulers, false teachers, corrupt political leaders, abusers, deceivers, and abortionists, are experiencing more intense suffering. Even though rapists, pedophiles, and adulterers cannot have sex, they go through the motions, which no longer gives them any pleasure. Addictions people substituted for God on earth continue to play out in hell. Here, everyone suffers differently according to their choices on earth. Just as we chose the way we lived on earth, so our suffering is dictated by those sinful earthly choices. You could say our suffering is tailor-made by our desires, preferences, priorities, and pursuits on earth. We didn't seek help from God for deliverance while on earth, and so we continue in our bondage, which followed us here.

I never realized how much love I needed until I entered this place, which was devoid of the love of God and friends. God promised **joy** to

His people, but we only experience sadness, pain, and suffering. God talks about people in heaven experiencing **peace**; we experience turbulence, crying, and fear. God offers His people **hope**; now, we exist without ANY hope for our future. God is **light**, but He shares no light here; we are surrounded and indwelt with darkness. God is **good**, but He withholds all goodness from all in this place. God made all believers members of His **family**, but there is no sense of family or unity with anyone here. Christians became God's **friends**, and we remain His enemies. There were stories of terrifying creatures on Earth, but we only saw them in our imagination. Those creatures are here, and the intensity of their terror is horrifying.

Torment

In Jesus' account, all He said about me was, *"In Hades, where he was in torment[2]...."* Later, he quoted me when I said I was in agony.[3] Torment is a generous description. Existence here unrelentingly sucks the life out of you. You want your life to end, but realize this existence will continue forever. It would be best to rid yourself of any idea that some have used to describe hell by saying they will always party because all their friends will be with them. Many of my friends are here, and we all discovered that self-centered people in pain care more about themselves than others. They experience regret, pain, and guilt because of their sins, and the worst fire is within our being, for that is the source of our sins. The fire continues to execute judgment on our imagination, conscience, heart, and tongue. That is where I feel so

---

[2] Author's note: 'As I seek to explain the kind of torment and agony Jokim experienced, I focused on the various meanings of torment and agony. I then thought of how one's life experiences would be the source of specific pain, regret, and suffering. If unbelievers are going to suffer for their sins, then the suffering is specific to the kinds of sins committed in life.' **Torment** is from basanos and similar Greek words and means severe pain associated with torture and torment, severe suffering. Odýnē – a related word – means physical pain and mental distress. Odynáō is "to cause pain or sorrow, to feel pain, to suffer.

[3] **Agony** in Greek means anguish of heart, sorrow, distress of body and mind, grieved, consuming grief. Hebrew equivalent: Sudden terror,-horror, anxiety, deep grief of the soul, pangs of conscience, the torment of eternal loss, the anguish of remorse, the sorrow of separation from friends and loved ones

much pain and torment. I never considered that my torment would be so targeted.

I struggle with the question, "Why doesn't God release us at some point?" I've come to realize that it's because we rejected that inner awareness that God implanted in us that we are eternal beings and that our actions on earth would have everlasting effects. God also declared in His word that we needed to make sure we were right with him instead of handing over the care of our souls to others, even though they were well-meaning family members or friends. He sent people into our lives to talk about meeting God at the reservation desk, but we ignored them or discounted the importance of the message they sought to share with us. Oh, I wish I had listened. Unlike you, I actually heard Jesus talk about these issues when He was in Jerusalem.

The Experience of Torment

I used words and phrases a moment ago to describe the sufferings of this place, but let me go into more detail about the kinds of anguish I experience here. First, we do not experience torment the same way every day, and it is not constant or consistent. It comes in waves, and there is constant variation. Think about life on earth. Some days were better than others. Some days, one thing bothers you, and another day, something different disturbs you. Some days we were carefree and joyful. Then, some days were absolutely horrifying when everything seemed to come crashing in on you at once. Suffering, pain, and agony come in various ways here as well. For instance, people who go to heaven have heightened use of their senses; we also have that here in hell. We have a greater sensitivity to the evil and pain around us by understanding the reason for our pain and sense of loneliness and the separation from God and good friends.

Total Recall

I now have an excellent memory; I recall every event in which I was involved and every word I spoke accompanied with my intent. I remember every sinful detail about how I treated people and everything

I did or experienced. My actions and words torment me, but my motives and attitudes become vivid reminders of how I showed contempt for people and took advantage of them. It's not like my memories are just shadowy thoughts; my mind relives each event with vivid, full-color details.

As I remember my actions and words, I become totally aware again of how I armed my attitudes and motives with barbed insults and calculated reactions. I saw how my vile, sinful nature expressed hatred, contempt, jealousy, greed, and pride as I sought to build myself up by tearing someone down. Back then, I was proud of how I could humiliate someone or get the best of them, but now it only brings me pain. To escape that sudden grip of guilt now, I go into protection mode and justify my past actions. Exposing my so-called wrongs is like touching an exposed nerve, creating pain and anger.

When I helped others, I was reminded that my actions were more a pretense than seeking to meet the other person's needs. I now see every lustful thought and sexual encounter with those women at our feasts in a different light. I understand how I reinforced their hurts from past sexual violations done to them. I see how it made the woman feel dirty and unworthy to approach God. I gave her a wrong understanding of the sanctity of sex and God's desire for how sex is to be a good and holy part of life. Women became objects of my desire rather than ones to be cherished, honored, and protected. The thoughts of how I violated and hurt those women constantly torment my soul. I didn't realize how unrestrained feelings of guilt could haunt me so much here. That is part of my burning, unrelenting torment.

My thoughts often wandered to my treatment of these women and how wrong it was. You would think that I would have tremendous regret. That, however, does not continue very long. Even the pain of suffering doesn't soften my heart, and instead of yielding to regret, I respond in rage and lash out at God. Then something, I don't know what, perhaps God, closes my mouth, and the guilt of my actions brings torment to my soul. Even amid that torment, I find myself justifying my actions by blaming those women for being so willing to please me.

They're just as guilty as I am. It's not all my fault. Neither is it my fault that they continued on their path away from God because I offered them money to meet with me. It's their fault because I don't think my influence had anything to do with them turning from God. My thoughts go back and forth, from regret with tears to justifying my actions and responding in rage. Double-mindedness is a part of the torture I experience.

These embedded thoughts constantly replay what I did wrong and how much I hurt these women and dragged them further off the right path. But I can't stop justifying my actions and the pleasure I had. I realize, like David, that my sins against these women and every other sin were an offense against God.[4] Passages of Scripture that I learned from my youth exposed why my actions were so sinful. That is how my regret and guilt burn within me every day. My sexual acts outside of marriage may captivate my mind for a week or a month, and then something else will come to mind, and I will be stuck on that one thought, like a stuck record that keeps playing the exact phrase repeatedly. On earth, I buried my wrong actions in the recesses of my thoughts and my comfortable but busy life. However, I can't avoid the torment of my wrong here. Torment invades my whole being every time I recognize the evil of what I did, how it offended God, and how it hurt the person or persons I violated, harmed, or influenced. Choosing to place my selfish wants before the needs of others continue to cause remorse. That fuels my burning torment.

Suffering Doesn't Change My Heart

Even though I suffer from these sinful actions, it doesn't change my heart. Regret or remorse do not always control me. [5]I continue to

---

[4] *"For I know my transgressions, and my sin is always before me. Against you, you only, have I sinned and done what is evil in your sight; so you are right in your verdict and justified when you judge."* (Psalm 51:3-4 NIV) This caused David to repent, but Jokim to experience the continual agony of his sins.

[5] *"Let the one who does wrong continue to do wrong; let the vile person continue to be vile; let the one who does right continue to do right; and let the holy person continue to be holy."* (Revelation 22:11 NIV) Vile and wrong are both in the present tense, indicating which

have an evil and deviant heart that justifies my actions and hates exposing the intent of my heart and actions. I liked the darkness, for it made me more comfortable engaging in those actions, even though I can only be involved in them through my thoughts.

Days of torment would turn into weeks as [6]I cursed and raged against God for condemning me to this terrible place. "Why didn't you see the good in me?" I shouted in anger. "Why is life so useless here? Couldn't you have provided a place like purgatory to purge my sins and then allow me into heaven? Why did you sentence me to this eternal condemnation in this god-forsaken place?"

Then it hits me; I'm in this god-forsaken place because I was the one who forsook God. It was my fault, not His, because I loved the darkness of my ways.[7] Whereas lies reigned on earth as people walked away from God, in this place where people are separated from God, truth assaults us with the reality of our sins, failures, faults, rejection, and immoral choices. Then, the guilt washes over me for my actions

---

indicates it is an action that will continue. Vile means moral uncleanness. They will continue to be vile, for their character will be forever fixed. Some think that those in hell will become better because of their suffering and torment, but according to 22:11, that is not the case. Even though they are tormented by guilt and remorse, they have evil hearts tormented by guilt and remorse, their evil heart that will not bow to God. Just as a person who is drawn into an addiction does not change because they know they are doing wrong, neither will the person in hell be able to change their heart. Notice 22:15 *"Outside are the dogs, those who practice magic arts, the sexually immoral, the murderers, the idolaters and everyone who loves and practices falsehood."* It does not just say they practiced these things, but they practiced these things and love lies. Their love binds their evil hearts in bondage through eternity.

[6] **Gnash the teeth**, is translated with the following terms: be furious, be in great pain, be terribly worried, living in intense anxiety, lamenting. One would gnash their teeth from indignation. Lamenting over being cast away from God's presence and blessings. The term is used in Acts 7:54: "When the members of the Sanhedrin heard this, they were furious and gnashed their teeth at him. (Stephen)" So, not only would gnashing of teeth be associated with the expression of pain, anxiety, and lamenting, and lamenting it is also an expression of rage against God. There will be many expressions of one's emotions in hell. There is the frustration of being cut off from the light of God's presence, living in darkness, and knowing the difference, and the regret of having refused it.

[7] "[19] This is the verdict: Light has come into the world, but people loved darkness instead of light because their deeds were evil. [20] Everyone who does evil hates the light, and will not come into the light for fear that their deeds will be exposed." (John 3:19-20 NIV)

and unfair accusations against God. A few times, I almost regretted not going to the reservation desk to prepare for eternity, but I am here because I chose my way above God's, and He is allowing me to live out the consequences of *my* choices. The reality of my choices rips me apart every time I speak against God or remember my deviant actions or constant fantasies.

Raging at God happens regularly here but is always followed by regret and recognition of my choice to reject God's new life brought through regeneration. In fact, sometimes I remember my brief glimpse of God at my judgment in heaven. He was really impressive, and in that moment I felt His hurt for how my offenses tore at His heart. Then, to my surprise, I actually found myself praising Him because I recognized his holiness and purity.[8] Then I think, 'What a strange thing I am doing from this cursed place. All I can do is acknowledge that this is the truth about God. Then I return to other perverted thinking and ranting that accuses God and justifies my sins.

[9]Guilt and grief over my sins cause remorse that I can't escape. Then shame comes on me like a flood of emotion that I can't control, nor do the tears bring any relief. The recurring nature of this all-consuming guilt and regret is like a worm gnawing in my mind that never quits. I was able to harden myself against this guilt on earth, but part of the suffering here is that I come to the full realization that I was made in the image of God and designed to live a holy life. I did not

---

[8] Philippians 2:10-11 "that at the name of Jesus every knee should bow, in heaven and on earth and under the earth, and every tongue acknowledge that Jesus Christ is Lord, to the glory of God the Father."Why should this not happen at various times through eternity?

[9] Jesus describes hell as a place where"**their worm never dies.**" One of the things he could be referring to is the gnawing of their guilty conscience. They suppressed their feelings of guilt on earth with their distractions, reasoning, busyness, and avoidance. In hell, they will not escape it, for like a gnawing worm in their conscience will constantly make them aware of their sinful rebellion against God. Also, they will continue to do wrong in the way they rant at God and curse Him for the punishment they encounter daily. Those in hell were not saved from the power and penalty of sin. In their resurrection body, their lust will burn like fire, desiring fulfillment that will never be satisfied, and their worm gnaws away at their conscience with guilt, and shame, causing agony at its worst. It is their fire and their worm. They cannot ever escape its torment. The gnawing of conscience and physical pain are descriptions of the punishment which affects the whole person.

value that aspect of my being during my earthly life. Nor did I realize how deeply my soul could feel anguish for my actions, let alone how constant that grief can rip into my soul. That is part of my burning torment. As much as I rage against God, I keep seeing both sides of my sin: the pleasure and regret caused by sin. On the one hand, I recognize that I missed out by not following His ways or making a reservation for heaven, and on the other hand, I rage against God for not accepting my ways by allowing me to do what I want.

That is not the only kind of suffering that burns within me in Hades. I regret my lost friendships. My wife followed me here, and sadly, my brothers and children ended up here because of my influence. I didn't realize how essential friendships and relationships were to me. Now, I'm discovering that friendships are a thing of the past life and are no longer experienced here. No one trusts you, and this place has no love or kindness. At best, it is always evident that people and evil spirits merely tolerate you. There is no desire to share with anyone or have pleasure together. It is a dismal place without laughter, shared friendships, or the joy of doing things together. Oh, how I remember joking with my brothers. We would laugh and tease one another. You know, I haven't heard any laughing here at all. Oh, I miss seeing a smile on a person's face, hearing an encouraging word, and feeling at peace with friends. All of that is gone in this place. That is also part of my burning torment.

I Didn't take the Afterlife Seriously

I've made many sad discoveries in hell that bring regret and torment into my life. I came to realize that living for myself did not take into account how I influenced others. I'm not just talking about the people I influenced daily, but generations after I died. You know I was shrewd, ruthless, and inconsiderate in my business dealings. I would brag to my friends and tell them how I treated people to get the best deal possible, and usually, I relentlessly berated their product for a better deal. I instilled in my friends that such business dealings weren't personal; it was just business. They followed my example, hurt many people, and caused financial loss to people just trying to make a living.

Another sad discovery is how my influence on others also fuels my torment. It was bad enough that my friends were influenced, but they inspired not just their children but further generations to continue to follow the example of my sinful actions and attitudes. I'm discovering that my past influence on people further torments me. As I continue to learn about the people I influenced and all the people they hurt, I find that this is causing me increasing distress and suffering. I used to think I was only responsible for my actions, but I've discovered that I'm suffering because of my influence, which has passed to further generations.

Those who think they are only responsible for their actions are stunned that they experience suffering for how they acted and treated their children, fellow workers, and customers. Then there is the harm some caused people through their drug addiction, alcoholism, their verbal, physical or sexual abuse, gossip, lies, and a myriad of other sins. As they learn how their sins influenced people's actions and thinking through the generations, it brings about more suffering. The consequences of the influence of their sins affect succeeding generations. I never dreamed that I would be suffering because I influenced my family and friends and those they influenced. Just like Adam's sin continues to impact generation after generation, our sins affect the following generations[10]. I continue to discover people my sinful actions have affected, which fuels my torment.

In my years here, I have continued to learn how my influence continued for generations. I passed on to my children and others how to

---

[10] **Romans 5:12:** *"Therefore, just as sin entered the world through one man, and death through sin, and in this way **death came to all people** because all sinned."* Adam's sin affects every person after him. **Exodus 20:5-6** *"You shall not bow down to them or worship them; for I, the LORD your God, am a jealous God, punishing **the children for the sin of the parents to the third and fourth generation of those who hate me**, ⁶ but showing love to a thousand generations of those who love me and keep my commandments."* When a person rejects God's way, they, in turn, impact those under their influence. We do not live in a vacuum, so our lives can have a continuing influence on others for many generations. (emphasis added by author)

show greed, disdain for lower-class people, and the priority of an immoral lifestyle. Because I did not value a genuine relationship with God, I have learned that each generation after me felt less need to acknowledge or follow God. They moved from just acknowledging God to being apathetic about him and finally distaining Him. The sins I chose to do in moderation, they eventually decided to do in excess.

I thought my life was my own and only needed to watch out for number one. That choice continues to cause me much agony as I observe how others who followed my example now suffer with me. Thinking only of myself blinded my eyes to the importance of serving others and providing an example for them to follow.

Thoughts of God were Recurring

I didn't realize how much I experienced God's love in all the beauty He created for us to enjoy. He allowed us to understand His love through our relationships with people, by people caring, forgiving, and encouraging us. Turning my back on God meant I turned my back on all the good God gave us on earth. I now see how His laws and teachings would have directed me into a much better way of life. Now, I'm feeling hollow because I'm not enjoying those benefits but am experiencing emptiness and loss for dismissing them from my life. I also feel the hurt that I brought into the lives of others.

You, my friend, are living the example others will follow. You will influence their decisions to either follow God or live for themselves. Knowing my life encouraged people to make the same determination I did about my relationship, and devotion to God has been a chief source of grief and torment. However, I have learned how to escape that guilt for a while. I say, "They were all responsible for their actions. They could choose to follow my example or do good. They are here because THEY decided to reject God. Don't blame that one on me. They followed me because they liked what they saw and wanted it too. My influence meant nothing!" As I said, that works for a while, but the reality is that I know it is a lie. Finding comfort in lies is our way of escape here, just as it was on Earth.

No Hope

If you are weary of hearing about my suffering, then realize that I have not yet begun to express the many facets of torment in this place. Every day I'm reminded that I chose this place to spend eternity. I get fixated on the term eternity and realize that it will continue forever and ever and ever and ever and ever and ever. You get the idea. You still have time to escape this place, but I can't because it is the destination I chose. I regret that I didn't take eternity seriously and visit the reservation desk before I died. I used my pursuit of wealth to consume my time so I didn't have to think about God and eternity seriously. Wealth became the god I served. I chose to focus on issues that only offered me personal gain and benefit in my earthly life, which allowed me to ignore critical life issues. Let me encourage you to regularly consider God, eternity, and how long your separation from God and good people will be if you reject reconciliation with Him. Every time I get upset over not being able to escape my guilty feelings for my wrongs, the thought comes to mind that this will never end. That is an inescapable part of my burning torment.

I'm often around people and spirits who are also in pain, as am I, and they don't cause me significant problems. Of course, arguments, name-calling, and bitter attacks exist, but I know that comes with the territory. We in hell don't have the kinder elements of our personality we had on Earth. Many think they are so much better than I am. Their discrimination continues to be motivated by jealousy, bullying, name-calling, and superiority. Yes, those sins continue to be very much alive and active here.

Horrors of this Place

What is most terrifying here are these frightening creatures called howling demons[11] that strike terror into our neighborhood. Remember,

---

[11] I developed this idea from the book, **DEMONS,** What the Bible really says about the powers of darkness. Michael S. Heiser, Lexhaam Press, P. 27

there are billions of people and beings here, so Hades is enormous. Like on Earth, there are cities and open spaces, but unlike Earth, the open spaces are drab and uninviting, and the cities have no beauty and are like the worst of slums.

Howling demons travel from place to place, inciting fear. As they invade each area, they bring an eerie kind of darkness that encompasses our environment and inner being. They are the most sadistic beings you could ever imagine. They have no shame in how they treat, demean, and abuse us. Inflicting pain and terror causes them delight and spurs them on. They are empty of any goodness. Every one of us in the area trembles when they make their rounds. Fear grabs every part of our being, and it is inescapable the entire time they are among us. There is no way we can prepare for the coming pain and terror. Even though we know it is coming, that does not lessen the effect of their terror. Their terrorizing is new each time and incites fear in ways we never experienced before. If you remember when bullies and mean kids tormented you unmercifully, you felt shame, insignificant, and had no good thoughts about yourself. You get only a tiny picture of how we feel when these vulgar howling demons torment us.

As time passed, I experienced enlightened thoughts. These beings I despised were actually like me. They just had more time to practice the depth of their depravity. We are kindred spirits; what I loathe in them is the same in me. Here in hell, we discover who we are when we turn our back on God and choose our way. I refused the new life God offered me, which meant I retained my sinful, rotten nature to dictate my existence. Just as Christians receive a new nature in the Holy Spirit and continue to grow in their understanding of God and develop their potential, we are allowed to experience the depth of our depravity in a civilization of beings on the same journey.

Here is a way to understand what this terror is like for us. Have you ever been out in the dark and suddenly heard a bone-chilling screech? Your mind conjures up all sorts of beings out there that can harm you. In the darkness, our fears grow in intensity. Just as fears were uncontrollable in our earthly bodies, they are more sensitive here.

The darkness that engulfs my soul during these times is so petrifying that I only think of the worst for myself. It takes several days and sometimes weeks for the memory of the howling demon's terror to abate. Then, after a year or two, I start thinking that it's about that time that they make their rounds, and I begin to wonder what new kind of terror they will inflict on me this time. Sometimes they will avoid a place for several years to keep people anticipating their coming. They know that suspense can be just as terrifying. No wonder Jesus calls this place outer darkness.

What I lost when I Chose Hell

The real pain is that what I lost by rejecting God's way of life was the ability to express the image of God. Do you remember when you desired to have something, such as food, to marry a particular person, or have the latest fashion in clothes, your first chariot, or maybe for you a new car? You wanted that so much that you could not sleep or think straight because it captivated your entire thought process, and you could not get it out of your mind. Here in Hades, you will have that same passion for expressing God's image in how you view life and relate to people, especially God. Here, I only have regret and all those feelings that cause torment and ignite pain. I gave up all the benefits of experiencing real life when I rejected God's provision of salvation.

Listen, friend, God made you in that image, and if you come here, His image in you will be like a raging lion seeking to be unleashed to express itself. You will experience nothing but remorse when you realize that you can never uncage that magnificent image and experience the riches of God's greatest blessings. The qualities of God's image in you in Hades are that it opens your eyes to the sinfulness of your life. That will burn in you like you never thought possible. You lose what would have been a wealthy life of experiences in the presence of God. That contributes to the burning torment. I discovered that as much as I rage against God, curse Him, and avoid the truth in my thinking, this is one truth that never goes away. It haunts me and is my greatest regret. Just as I sought to gain the most incredible wealth and treasures in life, I purposely neglected to pursue

God's life for me, and now the loss of that rages in me, causing intense regret. The reason for the rest of my guilt, I can temporarily find ways to justify my actions, but not for this loss.

My Neighborhood

That inner burning torment is only part of my agony in this horrible place. Living here is like living in the worst neighborhood, and there is no opportunity to move to a better part of town. It is a tormenting truth that I can't die. The pleasantness of life is something I no longer experience; even my neighbors look for ways to harm or abuse me daily. Even though some were very nice people on earth, they can no longer demonstrate goodness here. No one speaks a kind word. Then there are the evil spirits who practiced evil for thousands of years and know how to torment us unanticipatedly. They lash out at people in torment to quiet their inner agony. I wonder if I will become more like them as eternity progresses. Yes, we talk with them and seek peace so things can be a bit more pleasant. Our efforts work for a while, but there is always tension, knowing their evil desires are like a ticking time bomb in a James Bond movie. This place has no respect for truth, does not value kindness nor practices love, and is not a place of peace, joy, or comfort. You are correct in viewing this place as hell. The residents contribute significantly to the reality of dwelling in a place of constant burning torment.

I Can't Forget About God

I do miss the good times and realize they will never be a part of my existence, but my new normal is that I will always be surrounded by evil. That is a constant source of torment and suffering, making this an unbearable place to spend eternity. If you are thinking that, you would only be partially correct. The real issue is that I am not in God's presence and can no longer experience His glory. All of us here rejected the One who is Life.

I often think back to when I stood before God at my judgment. I remember the presentation of my life review vividly. It was God's case against me. What took me a lifetime to live was presented in just a short time. I knew I could make no defense for my actions, so I stood closed mouth[12] because I was guilty of disobedience, evil, and every sinful word and thought. In that time, I saw more than His righteous desire to be just in sentencing me; I also got a glimpse of His glory, love, and commitment to truth. He is such a beautiful God. I can see why people choose to be reconciled with Him and get to know Him. I never saw God as glorious as I did in those few moments before Him. Let me put it in terms you can understand. When I first met the woman who would become my wife, I could not think of anyone else from then on, and I knew I wanted her for my wife. She captivated my thinking and dreams of the future, and I just knew I wanted to be with her because of the joy we would have together. That's also how I felt when I saw God. I got that glimpse of Him in His glory, and I still can't get that picture out of my head.

Even when I struggle with my guilt and agony of the sins and failures I committed on earth and respond by cursing God and defaming His name, my heart now cries out to know this God I rejected. It is a curse to know the truth and realize that I chose lies instead. Even in Hell, I long to be with Him and experience His presence. I was designed and made to be with God and fulfilled in a relationship with Him. On that Day of Judgment, I realized I had lost the one who wanted to be my best friend forever. Truly my BFF. If I did not see God like that, I would have gone to hell ignorant of what I was missing. However, seeing God created a desire in me that can never be fulfilled.

Wrong Priority

At that moment, I realized what I had done wrong. I devoted myself to becoming rich, and in doing so, I sunk into poverty. I

---

[12] "Now we know that whatever the law says, it says to those who are under the law, so that every mouth may be silenced and the whole world held accountable to God. (Romans 3:19 - NIV)

committed myself to gaining wealth, and in that pledge, I dedicated almost every waking hour to thinking, dreaming, and serving that desire. I was willing to sacrifice for my cause of gaining more riches. I talked with people about business deals and how to make more money. It dominated almost every conversation. I pursued wealth for the prestige it gave me and the opportunities to gratify my fleshly desires. All the energy I used to focus on wealth as the meaning of my life is what God deserved from me. He deserved my time, thoughts, and willingness to sacrifice for Him, develop a holy life, and help others like Lazarus. I should have talked with people about God rather than money. I should have expressed my excitement to others about God and knowing Him. Life is about knowing God, and then the rest of life falls into place. Here, I will never experience God in that way.

Idolatrous greed fueled my focus on wealth and the desire to be recognized by others. That may not be your focus, but yours may be sensuality, fame, power, position, pleasure, politics, sports, intellectualism, or extreme challenges. To what are you giving the majority of your time in your imagination and actions? For what are you willing to sacrifice? On what do you focus your thinking and dreams? These are good until we make them the sole focus of our lives, thus leaving God out or placing Him in some subservient position. Let me tell you, there is nothing more important than God. You will learn that very early in eternity, whether in hell or heaven.

Let Me Paint a Better Picture for You

What was that? Excuse me for a moment. I have to talk to the big boss.

My supervisor helped me realize I was getting sentimental with you. My boss, Satan, reminded me of what is crucial. What I said was uncomfortable for you to hear, but you get used to it after a while. I want to extend a heartfelt invitation for you to join me. God paints such an awful picture of this place. I get so upset with Him because He thinks He's the only God, and nothing rivals **HIS** heaven. God thinks He's so good with all that love and forgiveness and making you part of

His family. Why doesn't He leave everyone alone to make their own decisions about where they will spend eternity?

It would be best if you remembered that this is a popular place for your eternal existence. More people end up here than in heaven, so you'll be with the popular crowd, and I'm sure you will be as comfortable as the next person. Just make sure you avoid that Reservation Desk, or you might end up in that **OTHER** place. He may tell you all kinds of good things about heaven, and they may be the truth, but this is the popular place where almost everyone else will hang out. We have your favorite singers, actors, sports stars and intellectuals here. I hope you will continue your journey in the way you are going so you can join all the rest with me here at the end of your life.

Excuse me. It seems like my business-dealing side just got the best of me, and I had to try to persuade you to come to this place. Let's get off this rabbit trail, and I'll proceed with my story.

8.   I Saw Abraham and Lazarus (Verses 23-26)

I DON'T KNOW how long I was living in torment. Adjusting took a while, and I got over those initial regrets of wondering why this was happening. In a new place, you only look at your initial surroundings, and then, as you become familiar, you start to explore to see what else is there. As you noticed in my description of this place, it is not pleasant, and there was nothing to attract me to any part of it, not even my old friends.

I Looked Up

Then, one day, I did something I had not considered doing since I arrived. I looked up. I blinked my eyes a few times in surprise. Was I seeing things, or was my mind playing games with me? Above me was Abraham looking down, and who was by his side but Lazarus. Wooo. I shouted a greeting to him, and to my surprise, he responded pleasantly. It was so good to communicate with someone who spoke with kindness. I will always cherish that one friendly greeting, even if I never hear it again. I don't know if I'll be able to do this again in Hades or if this kind of opportunity will be available when I'm in the lake of fire.

I was confused and stammered a bit, wondering what to say. It shouldn't be hard to think of something. After all, since I arrived, life has been full of heartache, pain, and suffering. So I blurted out the thing that consumed me every day: *"Father Abraham, have pity on me and send Lazarus to dip the tip of his finger in water and cool my tongue because I am in agony in this fire."*

I lived in a place where no one showed any pity, and there was no relief from suffering. Hell's residents are as self-centered as I am. Just to hear a pleasant voice and someone who cared about me would mean so much, so I asked Abraham to show me pity.

Why did I ask him to send Lazarus? It wasn't that we were friends. After all, I just showed him contempt and extended him no help. I looked down on him and saw him as worthless and an eyesore. Here comes one of those regrets in my thinking. Why did I think Lazarus would do anything for me because I certainly deserved no help or recognition from him? Notice I did not ask Lazarus for help. My feeling of superiority never left me. The status of this man was that of a servant, so I asked him to serve my desire for relief. I would never consider asking Abraham to help me. Indeed, he is a man of authority and could command Lazarus to grant my request.

Water

Your next question may be, "Why did I ask for water?" If water is needed to exist in hell, there would be sufficient water there. The spirit beings there would certainly not need water, for water is needed only for physical bodies. People in hades or hell don't have the same kind of physical bodies they had on earth. Is there a need for water to exist here? If not, why did I ask for just a drop of water on my tongue?

Remember that physical water is not the only kind of water. Jesus spoke of the living water to the woman at the well in John 4. I also heard Him speak of it when I attended the feast that John writes about in John *7:37-39 "On the last and greatest day of the festival, Jesus stood and said in a loud voice, "Let anyone who is thirsty come to me and drink. Whoever believes in me, as Scripture has said, rivers of living water will flow from within them." By this, he meant the Spirit, whom those who believed in him were later to receive. Up to that time, the Spirit had not been given, since Jesus had not yet been glorified."*

The living water is the indwelling presence of the Holy Spirit who empowers the believer to live the new life, that is, to express more fully the image of God placed in them. That image of God in me that I long to express causes me incredible frustration and regret because I no longer have the capacity to experience it. Out of desperation, I call on Abraham to allow the one who expressed that image to others to come and give me a taste of what God desired me to have.

Abraham's response crushed me. He said, "it was not within his ability to allow Lazarus to come to help me. There is a reason for the separation between us. By your lifestyle, you chose what was important to you, and he chose what was important to him. He chose God's way, and you did not, and that causes this separation."

Then Abraham went on to tell me why Lazarus could not come to help me. "God set the divide in place so no one can cross from one side to the other. Never again will there be a mingling of those who love God and those who have shown hatred and contempt for God by rejecting Him. Jesus said, "He that is not for is against me." (Matthew 12:30) And never is that more apparent than at death. God will not allow his world to be contaminated with sin again." [13]

No Escape

Abraham stated that there is no escape from eternal punishment. There have been escapes from prison and dangerous situations, but there will never be an escape from Hades or the Lake of Fire. Humans always think they can worm their way out of a precarious place. The question is this, 'Where will they go?' They can't escape God. God won't accept them into heaven. Another thing some don't consider is that God will take away all desire to escape the place because they know they deserve what is happening to them.

Another concept came into my mind as I raced to look for him to do something else for me. If I can see the other side now, in Hades, will we also be allowed to see the other side when we are in the Lake of Fire? That would constantly remind us of what we lost by rejecting

---

[13] Revelation 21:27: "Nothing impure will ever enter it, nor will anyone who does what is shameful or deceitful, but only those whose names are written in the Lamb's book of life."

God and His salvation. It would make our suffering even worse to look up and see people, loved ones, and friends enjoying life to the full. It would be pleasant to hear people laughing, singing, joking, and praising God. None of that goes on here. Maybe God will be merciful enough not to allow us these glimpses of heaven.

Rewards

This sighting was not the only time I saw Abraham. It happened many decades or so later that I saw Abraham again. Lazarus was not with him. So I inquired about where he was. Abraham filled me in on some of what was happening in Lazarus' life. There was a grand reward ceremony, and God honored him. He received the reward for faithfully enduring and the crown of life.[14] Because of his faithfulness, God gave him a position of ruling over five cities.[15] He is highly honored by those in his town. Lazarus is also a great teacher about God's goodness and faithfulness to those who live by faith.

UNBELIEVABLE! I couldn't wrap my head around what I was hearing. As my anger welled up within me, I went into a rage. I was ready to spit nails, and I couldn't help but curse that man. How could God honor such an impotent, worthless, insignificant person? I worked hard, built an empire, and developed relationships among those in authority. God put that helpless, inconsequential person in charge of something I could manage much better. I am better equipped than he could ever be. How could God honor him above me? It's like all that I accomplished meant nothing. Why did God not honor me? As I asked that question, suddenly, it hit me. God did not honor me because I did

---

[14] "Blessed is the one who perseveres under trial because, having stood the test, that person will receive the crown of life that the Lord has promised to those who love him." (James 1:12 - NIV) See also Revelation 22:12, 1 Corinthians 9:24-25, 1 Thessalonians 2:19-20, 2 Timothy 4:7-8, 1 Peter 5:1-4.

[15] "The first one came and said, 'Sir, your mina has earned ten more.' "' Well done, my good servant!' his master replied. 'Because you have been trustworthy in a very small matter, take charge of ten cities.' "The second came and said, 'Sir, your mina has earned five more.' "His master answered, 'You take charge of five cities.' (Luke 19:16-19 NIV) See also Rev 5:10, 20:6, 22:5; 2 Timothy 2:12

not honor Him. My priority was earthly wealth, fame, and power. I dismissed God's eternal wealth, valued glory among humanity rather than God, and neglected the power to live a righteous life to honor God.

I HATE THIS LIFE! Whenever I learn more about how I lived my life, it drives me into a rage and uncontrollable ranting for days. Then something happens after a time. God then opened my understanding of how my life dishonored Him, bringing me a fresh wave of guilt that I must continually endure. You know life is hell here, and it just doesn't improve. But that's enough camel chasing. Let me get back to my story about when I first saw Abraham and Lazarus.

Then It Came to Me

My mind was racing to figure out how to take advantage of this situation and get something. I had retained my ability to pursue aggressively what I wanted. I was not one to give up quickly because I have always been driven to get my way. Then it came to me. If Lazarus couldn't come here to help me, perhaps there is another kind of favor he could grant me. "Father Abraham, could you….

Daniel 12:2

"Multitudes who sleep in the dust of the earth will awake some to everlasting life, others to shame and everlasting contempt."

Matthew 25:46

"Then they will go away to eternal punishment, but the righteous to eternal life."

Jude 6-7

"And the angels who did not keep their positions of authority but abandoned their proper dwelling—these he has kept in darkness, bound with everlasting chains for judgment on the great Day. "*In a similar way, Sodom and Gomorrah and the surrounding towns gave themselves up to sexual immorality and perversion. They serve as an example of those who suffer the punishment of eternal fire.*"

9.   Send Him to My Brothers (Verses 27-31)

WE DON'T LOSE OUR MEMORY of life on earth when in the eternal state. What benefit would that be to suffer or be honored for unknown reasons? I despised Lazarus, and I remembered him. My brothers are far more important to me. As the thought of my brothers came to me, I was concerned like never before. I had so many good times with them, and I loved them. I don't want my example to be something they followed and ended up here with me.

I remember my plea to Abraham like it was yesterday. "Oh, please let Lazarus go and talk to them. Yes, I'm begging you, Abraham. That's something I never had to do. People usually begged me for something. Oh, this is so humiliating. I've always been so self-sufficient and independent, and now I'm asking you to do my bidding and help me in a very critical situation. Father Abraham, certainly Lazarus, has nothing better to do, so send him to my brothers. I don't want them to come to this place of torment. It is more than I can stand, so I certainly don't want them to follow me here. Father Abraham, I'm showing concern, doesn't that count for something?"

But I learned that my goodness now doesn't erase my sins. I decided to enter eternity with an unpaid debt that only God could pay. My self-sufficiency left me indebted for eternity. I own my actions, and now my situation is a real bummer.

Abraham's response was not what I wanted to hear. '*They have Moses and the Prophets; let them listen to them.*' We never thought those prophets were all that important as we grew up, so there's no reason to believe my brothers will listen to them now. They are like I was and didn't realize what was at stake. They've already written the prophets off and won't listen to them. They need something new and novel. They need to see someone who came back from the dead. I think that will make them wake up and listen. Most importantly, turn to God to receive salvation. Please, Abraham, there's nothing more important. Please help me by getting the message of redemption to them.

I'm sure that if someone returns from the dead, they will listen. Why wouldn't my brothers listen? How can they deny a miracle, especially one who has risen from the dead? I know they will sit up and listen; perhaps some will repent of their willful rejection of God.

I was grasping at straws. I was ready to do anything. I had nothing to offer Abraham. I felt helpless. I was begging him, hoping he would have mercy on me. But I could not move him to act on my brother's behalf. Never before have I made such an impassioned plea for something, or should I say, someone. I want to help them. I can't just stand here and do nothing. It's like watching my family trapped in a burning building, and I can't do anything to save them. I know their misery is coming, and I'm helpless to inform them of their impending judgment. Abraham, is there nothing that you can do for them?

As I look back on this moment, I see the fallacy in my thinking and understand why Abraham said what he did. I comprehend his response because I wonder if even I would have listened if Lazarus had returned from the dead. I would have just said, "This useless man has returned to torment me, and I would not have considered the miracle that brought him back.

Do you want to know what he told me? *"If they do not listen to Moses and the Prophets, they will not be convinced even if someone rises from the dead."* God's word is the message to all humanity. He expects us to take Him seriously, to recognize who He is and what He did for us. The Bible reveals us as sinners who need redemption and reconciliation with God. He expects us to acknowledge the authority of His word about having a relationship with Him and how we are to live.

This Is What I Was

If you want to know the kind of person I was, you could compare me to the Pharisees. I was self-righteous and sought to justify all the actions that allowed me to continue my sinful lifestyle. When the Pharisees learned Jesus rose from the dead, they sought to cover it up rather than see the glory of God and what He wanted us to learn from this man dying and raised to life. I remember talking with some Pharisees, and they were doing everything they could to hide the truth of His resurrection. I even gave them an idea or two because I was on their side. They saw undeniable resurrections, so what makes me think that my brothers would change even if they saw Lazarus return to life and bring a message from their brother to repent because God's judgment awaits them?

My life had a negative influence on my brothers. They are now here in Hades with me. Jesus gave you a glimpse of my life to show where you will end up if you have not trusted Jesus to become your savior. He wants you to have a happy ending to your life as you live with Him. Just as I chose not to go to the other Reservation Desk to accept God's salvation, you now have that decision to make. Will you choose yourself and your way above God? Will you choose hell instead of heaven? Will you choose a life of torment and suffering instead of joy and love? Will you choose a place of anguish or peace? There is a hell or lake of fire, and there is God's heaven. There will be vile, unfriendly people in hell, but you have the holy angels, saints, and God in heaven. You are the one who decides your destination.

I thought I had a lot more time to decide to get right with God. Be mindful not to let the pleasures of this life blind your mind to the issue of where you will spend eternity, as I did. If you choose sinful pleasures and your own way above God's, then you reject God's eternal pleasures, joy, love, peace, and fellowship with Him. This is the most important of all your choices on earth.

Ignoring the issue of hell and my eternal destiny did nothing to make it disappear or take care of itself. Hiding behind intellectual reasoning by saying there is no hell does not change what will happen to you. The only way you can know about what happens after death is for someone to reveal what is to come. On what authority are you basing your rejection of hell? Do you think God will exempt you from having your own life reviewed and judged before you enter eternity? Would you please take these issues seriously?

If I could come back from the dead, I would do everything I could to dissuade you from coming to where I spent the last 2000 years. It is a real place of regrets that never ends. I beg you, and I urge you not to follow me here. However, the choice is yours alone. What will you do about your future?

GO!

Now scram. Get out of here. I'm tired of having people come to see me, then walk away, and not allowing my example to make a difference in their lives. They still don't take the reality of this place seriously. They think they aren't that bad, and their good works will cover their sins. The truth is that I see myself in you, and I know all the regret it has caused me over the years. Go ahead and leave. I'm tired of seeing your face, but I know many will come down here anyway, and I'll see you for eternity. Why don't people learn? Their self-centeredness has such a hold on them. If you're not right with God and want to spend eternity with me, I have one final word of advice for you. Don't go to the other Reservation Desk. They will take away your dignity by saying that your good works will do nothing to get you right with God, and they will offer you salvation as a gift. Keep your pride and shame, avoid the Reservation Desk, and join me here. Perhaps we will meet again for a loooonger visit.

10. Reservation Desk

> *Perhaps you are not interested in choosing to become a neighbor of Jokim. Then, allow me to point you to the Reservation Desk where you can cancel your reservation for hell and become a citizen of heaven and a child of God. That's the only way you can change your destiny. (John 14:6, 5:24, 6:47; 1 John 5:11-12)*

"Welcome. May I help you?"

"Yes, I would like to make my reservation for heaven. I don't want to go to that other place, so I wanted to reserve a place in heaven."

"Well, you've come to the right place. There's lots of room, and we have the best accommodations in the entire universe. I'm always glad to see people coming to this line instead of that long line for hell. It's not a good place, but it is trendy and large. They have hundreds of more reservation clerks there than we have here. Anyway, I enjoy taking my turn here at the desk often, and I think you'll find our destination more pleasant than the 'other place.'"

"That sounds good. What does it cost to go to heaven? I want you to know that I've been a good person most of the time. But I must admit that there have been some lies, moral failures, and cheating on my taxes in life. Besides, I'm like most people; I've been pretty good."

"You sound like a fine applicant. We always enjoy having sinners come to make a reservation for heaven."

"You make it sound like my sins are worse than I think. I told you I'd done many good things in life, and I'm sure they make up for the sins I've committed."

"Many people get hung up on that issue. Let me ask you a couple of questions. They will help you see your need for making the proper reservations. The first question is this, 'Have you ever lied?'"

"Well, yes, I have. Everyone lies, and I'm no worse than the rest of the people I know."

"Let me show you how serious even one lie is. The Bible lists those who will enter the lake of fire; you know, that's the long line over there that most blindly choose. Now, notice what Revelation 21:8 says, *"But the cowardly, the unbelieving, the vile, the murderers, the sexually immoral, those who practice magic arts, the idolaters **and all liars**— they will be consigned to the fiery lake of burning sulfur. This is the second death."* (NIV) You have already acknowledged that you are a liar, which means you need to be reconciled with God, and we offer that service here. Now, you may reason, 'Yes, I've sinned, but I'm not that bad.' I'm correct in that statement because you already told me you lie. The truth allows you to recognize that you are a sinner who needs reconciliation with God or salvation from the penalty of sin. If you are ever going to die, then you are a significant enough sinner to need salvation or reconciliation. The apostle Paul reminds us of this truth. *"Therefore, just as sin entered the world through one man, and death through sin, and in this way death came to all people because all sinned."* Romans 5:12 (NIV).

"You sure got me on that last one. I can deny that I'm a sinner for many reasons, but that verse sure put me in my place. In my pride, I could argue with you, but I think you know what you're talking about, so I agree with you that not only am I a sinner, but bad enough to need to get right with God."

"Good for you, for you are among a small group that knows you are a sinner and that you need to get right with God. Every person fits into that category, but few will admit it."

"Thank you; honesty is important if you want to resolve an issue."

"The next part of the application for entrance into heaven is this. That sin you just admitted is sufficient reason for God to sentence you to hell. Your sins are a blatant offense against the holy God of heaven. He, therefore, must punish sin by separating a person from Him for eternity."

"Wow! I didn't know it was that serious. I thought God accepted most people who were pretty good but not those who were extremely evil. That accusation against me sure would have surprised me when I stand before God one day. So first, I acknowledge I'm a sinner and deserve God's holy punishment for my willful sin. I'm on board with that. No arguments or denials from me."

"It's always good to see a person get their thinking on the right track. Let's move along to the next point. That penalty of sin you deserve can never be paid, not even in hell. That's why there's no end. No one can make sufficient payment ever to exit hell. However, there is good news in all of this. God loved humanity so much that he made a deal with his Son, Jesus Christ, to come to earth, live a perfect life, so he had no penalty against him, and then die as a sacrifice for our sins, thus making full payment for our debt that made us God's enemy. Listen to these wonderful words, *"But God demonstrates his own love for us in this: While we were still sinners, Christ died for us. Since we have now been justified by his blood, how much more shall we be saved from God's wrath through him! For if, while we were God's enemies, we were reconciled to him through the death of his Son, how much more, having been reconciled, shall we be saved through his life!"* Romans 5:8-10 (NIV). Before we approached God for help, He provided humanity's only means of salvation."

"You mean someone who never did anything wrong took my punishment so I wouldn't have to suffer in hell?"

"You are correct. You owed a debt you could not pay, and Jesus paid a debt He did not owe so that you could be with him in heaven. Listen to the words of Jesus, *"My Father's house has many rooms; if that were not so, would I have told you that I am going there to prepare a place for you? And if I go and prepare a place for you, I will come back and take you to be with me that you also may be where I am."* John 14:2-3 (NIV) Reconciliation with God makes you a member of his family, and he will bring each of His children home to live with him for eternity. Not a bad deal, huh?"

"That is fantastic. That's better than what I expected. I came here to make reservations for heaven, so what do I need to do to earn a ticket?"

"This is where many people get confused, so let me start by using a comparison. If you want a new computer and go to the Best Buy store, what does it take to allow you to leave the store with it?"

"I would pull out my credit card and flop it down and say, 'Make it mine buddy, I'm paying for it.'"

"You understand that principle of buying. If you want something, you have to pay for it."

"The second part of the question is this. Suppose you wanted that same high-speed computer and tell your family that's what you want for Christmas. When it comes time to open gifts, they present you with your gift, and you know it is the computer you want. What are you going to do with your gift? Are you going to pull out your wallet and pay them for it? Will you think that you have to work off the debt in the future to deserve it? Or will you accept it as a gift as your family intended?"

"I know enough that you don't pay for a gift. You have to receive it, unwrap it and enjoy using it. I would rather get a gift like that than pay for it with my hard-earned money."

"With that in mind, I want to quote some verses, and you tell me how you gain reconciliation or salvation from the penalty of your sins. *"For it is by grace you have been saved, through faith—and this is not from yourselves, it is the gift of God—not by works, so that no one can boast.* Ephesians 2:8-9 (NIV). Grace is the favor we receive that we don't deserve. It is unearned but given freely. Then come the words in the verse, '*it is the gift of God.*' Let's return to our computer illustration. Do you pay for a gift or receive it because someone else paid for it?"

"Are you saying what I think I'm saying? Do you mean salvation is something I don't work for but receive as a gift?"

"Bingo! Bullseye, Right on! You Aced it, buddy. That simple concept is the most difficult for humans to comprehend. Let me read you a couple of other verses that affirm this truth. When talking about salvation, John said, "*Yet to all who did receive him, to those who believed in his name, he gave the right to become children of God.*" John 1:12 (NIV) Notice the terms used to reveal how to become a child of God. *Receive him* and *believe in his name.* Receive Him talks about the act of acceptance, and the word believe refers to trust to become His child. Isn't that part of receiving a gift? It is no longer a gift if you don't accept the gift. If you don't believe the gift is yours, then you will never use it. Part of the process is to receive Jesus willingly."

"You know, I've always made it so much more complicated than that in my mind. I always thought it would be more complex, which prevented me from figuring it out. Even when I trusted in all my good works, I never knew if and when I did enough to gain God's favor. So, I know all these truths, I'm a sinner, and there is a penalty for my sins, and Jesus paid sin's penalty when he died on the cross, and God offers me salvation as a gift. How do I finalize this deal with God?

"I will explain it to you with one final passage of Scripture. "*If you declare with your mouth, "Jesus is Lord," and believe in your heart that God raised him from the dead, you will be saved. For it is with your heart that you believe and are justified, and it is with your mouth that you profess your faith and are saved. For, "Everyone who calls on the name of the Lord will be saved.*" Romans 10;9-10, 13. "These truths about salvation are straightforward."

10:9

"Recognize Jesus is Lord. He's the only one capable of paying sin's penalty. Believe that He died and was raised from the dead. As you notice the truths presented in these verses, you recognize that salvation is both an act of faith or trust and an audible declaration of these truths. Paul goes on to explain the process in a little more detail."

10:10

"Believing comes from your heart. Your heart determines and expresses those beliefs. Believing that Jesus died and was raised from the dead is the basis of God's provision, so His payment of sins can be applied as payment for your sin debt. When you believe, which means that you fully place your trust in Jesus, then God justifies you. That means that God bases your acceptance on His act of justification. It is not your works that make you right with God but His unchangeable decree about you. Then, you need to declare your faith in Jesus for salvation openly. Those who do *believe and confess with their mouth are saved*. Salvation is not a list of dos and don'ts, but it means you enter into a relationship with God. That is why our hearts and voices are essential to this union with God. You no longer have to question if you belong to God and are right with Him."

10:13

"Do you know how you profess that faith with your mouth? You call on the name of the Lord. That means you pray and declare to God your trust in Him and ask Him to forgive you and save you from sin and its penalty. Prayer is like a conversation in which you are speaking to another person.

"Hey, thanks for telling me about that. You've been so kind and thoughtful. Say, I've been wondering about those scars on your wrists. How did you get those?"

"Those, my friend, are because of you when I died on the cross."

The Rich Man

"Jesus? **JESUS, IS IT YOU?!**"

"Yes, child, it is me."

"So, I don't have to wonder what you're like or if you're listening because you are right here in front of me."

"That's right."

"May I ask you to save me right now so I can be right with you?"

"I think I've explained it well enough, so tell me what you remember before you ask me."

"I'm so excited to be here with you. I don't want to be estranged from you another minute. Jesus, I don't know why you loved a sinner like me, but I am a sinner, and I know I've failed you so much. I deserve the penalty for my sins because you are holy. Thank you. **Thank You** for dying for me and paying for my sins. I believe in that truth with all my heart and ask you to be my Savior right now, and I welcome you into my life. Do I have to say Amen as people do after prayer?"

"No, son, that's enough. You expressed your heart, and now you are mine. Your decision begins a relationship journey where we walk together, live together, and accomplish great things for my kingdom. Let's start that journey.

James Olah August 28, 2021

"He said to me: "It is done. I am the Alpha and the Omega, the Beginning and the End. To the thirsty, I will give water without cost from the spring of the water of life. Those who are victorious will inherit all this, and I will be their God, and they will be my children." (Revelation 21:6–7, NIV)

~~~~~~~~~~~~~~~~

"The Spirit and the bride say, "Come!" And let the one who hears say, "Come!" Let the one who is thirsty come; and let the one who wishes take the free gift of the water of life." (Revelation 22:17, NIV)

~~~~~~~~~~~~~~~~

"Come, all you who are thirsty, come to the waters; and you who have no money, come, buy and eat! Come, buy wine and milk without money and without cost." (Isaiah 55:1)

"Seek the Lord while he may be found; call on him while he is near. Let the wicked forsake their ways and the unrighteous their thoughts. Let them turn to the Lord, and he will have mercy on them, and to our God, for he will freely pardon." (Isaiah 55:6–7, NIV)

~~~~~~~~~~~~~~~~
~~~~~~~~~~~~~~~~

11. Books on the Eternal State

These books are in paper and digital format, and some are available as audiobooks.

- **Glimpse into Heaven** by James Olah. This book offers you teachings and ideas to consider about the glories of heaven. Colossians 3:1-2 says, "Set your hearts on things above, set your minds on things above…." One aspect of that truth is to set your affection on God and your relationship with Him. But what will you do to enjoy God? What kind of things will you do to have fresh ideas of how to praise and worship God? This book offers you ideas of what life will be like there.

- **What in Hell is Happening?** by James Olah. This book offers more biblical insight into the character of hell and what people can anticipate. It also offers a different view of the fire or burning of hell.

- **Town of Salvation** by James Olah. This book presents the Gospel of Salvation in an easy-to-understand way. James starts by declaring that there are only two religions in the world. He then takes each religion to a town called Salvation and to the business or store, representing the work they claim to help them gain or maintain their salvation. Finally, he takes the Christians to the Gift Shoppe to show what is needed to receive their free gift of salvation.

- **Heaven:** *A Comprehensive Guide to Everything the Bible Says About Our Eternal Home*, by Randy Alcorn. One of this book's reviewers says: "Randy Alcorn's book on Heaven is a comprehensive treatment of the subject. Randy spent over 20 years researching the subject of Heaven as presented in the Bible. Heaven has been a neglected subject in churches for many years, and many claim death experiences that don't square with the Bible. This book is Bible-based and answers many questions we may have about Heaven."

- **Imagine Heaven**: Near-Death Experiences, God's Promises, and the Exhilarating Future That Awaits You, by John Burke. John seeks to base his writing on doctors or highly educated people who have nothing to gain by speaking of these stories. Some were skeptics when they first started hearing of these occurrences. Most became believers after a while. One of his reviewers says: "This book is excellent. It is compelling and awe-inspiring for anybody interested in NDEs (or Near-death experiences). The author has done a great job at compiling stats from hundreds of cases and has included excerpts from many to give the reader a real sense of what many people experience when they die and are brought back to life. It's hard to put down. There are many descriptions of Heaven and even a few horrible instances of hell."
- **HELL UNDER FIRE** by Christopher W. Morgan and Robert A. Peterson. The book is more of a scholarly work dealing with the many issues of the teaching of hell and also addressing the issues people use to oppose it.
- **Near-Death Experiences: To Hell and Back**: Real stories of people who had a near-death experience in Hell, by John Graden. It offers several stories about people who had Near-death experiences in hell.
- For other books the author published, search under his name, James Olah. His topics include a biblical view of suffering, Christian growth issues, and five titles on relationship concerns.

12. Bible Verses About Hell

Hell is not a place to take lightly. The Bible has many warnings of the terrors of hell and counsels us to avoid it at all costs. Many of these biblical warnings about hell are presented in this section.

Listen to this warning, and it is in your best interest to ensure you are right with God to avoid an eternity in hell. Many today seek to say there is no such place as hell, but here you read the words of Jesus, who is God, describing hell and calling you to avoid it. Before you go further, take a moment and talk to God, asking Him to open your eyes to the truths He wants you to learn.

Would you like your eye plucked out and your right hand cut off? Jesus says it's better to go through life without your significant body parts than to die and go to a fiery hell. Let's look at His teachings and warnings.

- If your right eye makes you stumble, tear it out and throw it from you, for it is better for you to lose one of the parts of your body than for your whole body to be thrown into hell. If your right-hand makes you stumble, cut it off and throw it from you, for it is better for you to lose one of the parts of your body than for your whole body to go into *hell*. Matthew 18:9
- If your eye causes you to sin, gouge it out and throw it away. It is better for you to enter life with one eye than to have two eyes and be cast into the *fiery hell*.
  Matthew 5:29
- If your right eye makes you stumble, tear it out and throw it from you; for it is better for you to lose one of the parts of your body, than for your whole body to be thrown into *hell*. Matthew 10:28
- If your eye causes you to stumble, throw it out; it is better for you to enter the kingdom of God with one eye, than, having two

eyes, to be cast into hell, *where their worm does not die, and the fire is not quenched.* Mark 9:43-48

Jesus teaches us that when we contemplate our relationship with God, we must remember His immense power and authority. As God, He is not to be taken lightly, for He does not tolerate those who turn away from His love and salvation. His commands are not mere suggestions but a testament to His sovereignty and our duty to respect and follow His will.

- Do not fear those who kill the body but are unable to kill the soul, but rather fear Him who is able to destroy both soul and body in hell. Matthew 5:22
- But I say to you that everyone who is angry with his brother shall be guilty before the court; and whoever says to his brother, 'You good-for-nothing,' shall be guilty before the supreme court; and whoever says, 'You fool,' shall be guilty enough to go into the fiery hell. Matthew 7:13
- "It is a dreadful thing to fall into the hands of the living God." Hebrews 10:31. Dreadful means someone who causes you to fear. He offers love to the whole world, and those who reject Him have something to fear.

When people devise their own way of salvation, it is always the wrong way. This way is wide because many choose a way not approved by God. Pride blinds their eyes to God's warnings so they find it easy to believe lies and avoid God's way. The wide way always leads to destruction. The narrow way is God's way. Jesus said "He is the way." There is NO other name given among men under heaven by which a person can be saved. This is the ONLY road that leads to life with God. There are many religious in the world, and they have all embraced different lies, and they have all rejected the same Truth. That doesn't mean that if a person is in the wrong religion they can't be saved. God doesn't save groups, He saves individuals. There are those in a religion that do not hold to God's way of salvation, but in that gathering, there are those who discover the truth, seek God, and are saved. Jesus said, "*I* *am the way, the truth, and the life; **NO one** comes to the Father except through Me."*

When speaking about both those going to be with Him, Jesus used the word eternal for the life believers have, and those who choose their own way will be cursed into eternal fire. The word **eternal** defines the duration of their existence. Jesus uses the same Greek word all three times. Twice it refers to eternal punishment and once to those with eternal life. **Eternal** means the same for both; it is forever. He makes that crystal clear. Seeking to make these words say something different is opposing God. Don't play word games with God; you can't win that battle. Reinterpretation does not change what God has said.

- "Enter through the narrow gate; for the gate is wide and the way is broad that leads to destruction, and there are many who enter through it. But small is the gate and narrow the road that leads to life, and only a few find it. Matthew 7:13-14

- Then he will say to those on his left, "Depart from me, you who are cursed, into the eternal fire prepared for the devil and his angels." Matthew 25:41

- These will go away into eternal punishment, but the righteous into eternal life." Matthew 25:46

- "Make every effort to enter through the narrow door; for many, I tell you, will seek to enter and will not be able. Once the head of the house gets up and shuts the door, and you begin to stand outside and knock on the door, saying, 'Lord, open up to us!' then He will answer and say to you, 'I do not know where you are from.' Then you will begin to say, 'We ate and drank in Your presence, and You taught in our streets.' But he will reply, 'I don't know you or where you come from. Away from me all you evildoers!' There will be weeping there, and gnashing of teeth…." Luke 13:24-28
It is not a pleasant thought to be part of those who will be among the multitude who do not know God. Notice the words used in the following verses, for they are unpleasant: "punished, everlasting destruction, shut out, smoke of their

torment, no rest day or night. These will not be part of those celebrating the coming of Jesus in his glory but are part of the group trembling in fear because their choices to reject Him are theirs to own for eternity.

- "He will **punish** those who do not know God and do not obey the gospel of our Lord Jesus. They will be punished with **everlasting destruction** and **shut out from the presence of the Lord** and the majesty of His power on that day he comes to be glorified in his holy people and to be marveled at among all those who have believed. 2 Thessalonians 1:8-10

- And the **smoke of their torment** goes up forever and ever; they have no rest day and night, those who worship the beast and his image, and whoever receives the mark of his name." Revelation 14:11

- And the devil who deceived them was thrown into the lake of fire and brimstone, where the beast and the false prophet are also; and they will be **tormented day and night forever and ever**. Revelation 20:10 *(Note: the beast and false prophet are humans. They will be tormented day and night forever. It is the fate of all who reject Jesus as savior.)*

- "But when the Son of Man comes in His glory, and all the angels with Him, then He will sit on His glorious throne. All the nations will be gathered before Him; and He will separate them from one another, as the shepherd separates the sheep from the goats; and He will put the sheep on His right, and the goats on the left." Matthew 25:31-33

- "Then He will also say to those on His left, '**Depart from Me, accursed ones, into the eternal fire** which has been prepared for the devil and his angels; Matthew 25:41 *(The author added the emphasis in verse.)*

The verses above indicate a separation will be made of humanity. No one will be overlooked or given another chance. Each individual chose the side on which they now stand before God. They can blame no one else but their selves for their eternal destiny, and God will affirm the decision they made before they died. Is this a decision you want to continue to put off?

Many people are revising their beliefs about hell. They look for ways to make it disappear or not mean what the Bible says. Their reinterpretation of the Bible is a way of changing God's words for the sake of making people feel safe, even though they're facing eternal danger when they die. When you read the final section of verses, you see that God is not playing games. Just as He is serious, you must be thoughtful about your eternal destiny. This final place, the lake of fire, is not a temporal assignment but an eternal penalty you must face if you are not right with God.

I recently read a book, "23 Minutes in Hell." Reading his description of hell in this experience turned my stomach, and I didn't want to continue reading. It terrified me. That was reading about his experience. It will be far worse if you choose to ignore God and thus decide to make the lake of fire your home for eternity. playing games with your soul is not wise.

- The Son of Man will send out his angels, and they will weed out of his kingdom everything that causes sin and all who do evil. They will **throw them into the furnace of fire**; in that place there will be **weeping and gnashing of teeth**. Matthew 13:42
- For if God did not spare angels when they sinned, but cast them into hell and committed them to pits of darkness, reserved for judgment.... Then the Lord knows how to rescue godly men from trials and to **hold the unrighteous for the day of judgment** while continuing their punishment...." 2 Peter 2:4-10
- You serpents, you brood of vipers, how will you escape the sentence of hell? Matthew 23:33
- And the sea gave up the dead which were in it, and death and Hades gave up the dead which were in them; and **they were judged, every one of them according to their deeds**. Then, death and Hades were thrown into the lake of fire. This is the second death, the lake of fire. And **if anyone's**

name was not found written in the Book of Life, he was thrown into the lake of fire. Revelation 20:13-15

- "The sons of the kingdom will be cast out into the **outer darkness**; in that place, there will be **weeping and gnashing of teeth**." Matthew 8:12
- Then death and Hades were thrown into the lake of fire. This is the second death, the lake of fire. Revelation 20:14
- "Again, the kingdom of heaven is like a dragnet cast into the sea, and gathering fish of every kind; and when it was filled, they drew it up on the beach; and they sat down and gathered the good fish into containers, but the bad they threw away. So, it will be at the end of the age; the angels will come forth and take out the wicked from among the righteous. Matthew 13:47-50
- Then another angel, a third one, followed them, saying with a loud voice, "If anyone worships the beast and his image and receives a mark on his forehead or on his hand, he also **will drink of the wine of the wrath of God**, which is mixed in full strength in the **cup of His anger**; and **he will be tormented with fire and brimstone** in the presence of the holy angels and in the presence of the Lamb. And **the smoke of their torment goes up forever and ever**; they have **no rest day and night**, those who worship the beast and his image, and whoever receives the mark of his name." Revelation 14:9-11
- *"God is just: He will pay back trouble to those who trouble you and give relief to you who are troubled, and to us as well. This will happen when the Lord Jesus is revealed from heaven in blazing fire with his powerful angels. [1]He will punish those who do not know God and do not obey the gospel of our Lord Jesus. [2]They will be punished with everlasting destruction and shut out from the presence of the Lord and from the glory of his might on the day he comes to be glorified in his holy people and to be marveled at among all those who have believed. This includes you, because you believed our testimony to you."* (2 Thessalonians 1:6–10, NIV)

1- Those who are punished are all who choose not to know and obey God. Good works don't get you into heaven, no matter how good they appear on Earth.

2- That everlasting destruction does not take them out of existence, for they are shut out from the presence of the Lord. Only a person who exists in an eternal state can be shut out. If a person goes out of existence, like many want to believe, then it is of no consequence to be shut out. There is a penalty for rejecting God and the opportunity He gave you.

As you contemplate these verses, don't write off Jesus' teaching or say that hell only refers to others and not me. Don't be naïve by thinking you're not that bad. Every person who will die is in need of salvation. Only sinners die. Will you be accepted? Jesus said, "Except a man be born from above, he cannot enter the kingdom of God.

"That if you confess with your mouth "Jesus is Lord," and believe in your heart that God raised him from the dead, you will be saved. For it is with your heart that you believe and are justified, and it is with your mouth that you confess and are saved. "Everyone who calls on the name of the Lord will be saved."

- - - - - - - - - - -

- *"When you face God on judgment day, He won't ask for your resume of good deeds. (Eph 2:8-9) Instead, He will check your birth certificate to see if you have been born again (John 3:3). Then, He will examine your passport to determine if you are a citizen of heaven (Philippians 3:20). What will you offer God on judgment day - your resume or your birth certificate?"*

"Almost every natural man who hears of hell flatters himself that he shall escape it; he depends upon himself for his own security; he flatters himself in what he has done, what he is now doing, or what he intends to do."

~ ~ ~ ~ ~ ~ ~ ~ ~ ~ ~ ~ ~ ~ ~

"It would be a wonder if some who are now present should not be in hell shortly before this year is out. And it would be no wonder if some persons who now sit here in this meeting house in health, and quiet and secure, should be there before tomorrow morning."

Jonathan Edwards – "Sinners in the Hands of an Angry God"

13.   Unquenchable Fire

Why does God speak of hell as a place of fire? Allow me to share an incident that opened up my understanding of a possibility as to why this term is used.

It all happened on a spring day when I decided to take about a decade of tax forms and receipts to the burn barrel to dispose of them. While burning the old tax papers, I noticed something interesting. You can't just put a paper bag full of documents into the burn barrel and think it will burn completely or quickly. It's like trying to burn a couple of books.

I placed a stack of papers into the burn barrel, and after a few sheets, it died down to a smolder. I wanted to get this job done, so I hung a couple of stapled sheets into the barrel this time. The one hanging sheet caught fire, and as I waited a moment, the rest became engulfed. As the fire grew, I continued to drop sheets into the barrel, and they caught fire quickly.

The more paper I placed in the barrel, the more it blazed until it became so hot that I had to step away. At this point, I made an important observation and discovered an answer to a burning question.

It occurred to me that fire is insatiable. It will continue to burn as long as it is fed. Sometimes, it burns down and smolders; other times, it roars. Fire is never satisfied. It will continue to burn as long as it has fuel. Over the years, I've heard of long-burning fires. I remember hearing in the news of a tire fire that burned for over a decade. At Yanatas in the Olympos National Park in Turkey, natural gas has burned from many vents on the side of the mountain for 2500 years. As long as a fire is fueled, it will burn.

This helped me to understand a crucial teaching in the Bible. When Jesus says people will be cast into hell and then into the Lake of Fire, I wondered why fire is used as the descriptive term to identify continual punishment. After all, hell was prepared for the devil and his angels. They are spirit beings, and physical flames only torment flesh. Then it came together for me. Hell is a place where torment is fueled by the guilt of our sins, the harm we've done to others, regrets, the recognition of our loss of usefulness, and our loss of relationship with God, who is the only source of life and meaning. That guilt never goes away because there is no forgiveness in Hell.

Guilt, regret, and every other reason for punishment will continue to be the cause of the gloom, despair, and agony that fuels the unquenchable nature of the fire of torment. Wave after wave will bring anguish to the inhabitants of the Lake of Fire. Their guilt, regret, and every sense of loss will feed the hurt as fuel feeds a fire. Never will their pain find relief. They have rejected God, and now they are alone. Their failures, attitudes, and conduct will continuously be relived in their minds as fuel for their distress. They will remember the hurt they brought on themselves as well as how they influenced others on Earth. Hell's occupants will not be able to write off their sinful actions, words, defiance, or attitudes that caused grief to themselves and others, for it will continue to bring them agony that is as insatiable as a roaring fire.

Every regret and pang of guilt their actions caused will burn in their memories, for they will continually remember it with pain and regret. That is why the fire is unquenchable: They will continue to experience their remorse for choosing sin rather than God and His goodness. This will haunt the unredeemed for eternity.

I think this is an explanation worth considering of why God uses the term fire to describe the torment of Hell or the Lake of Fire.

14. About the Author

James Olah is a retired pastor after having served for more than 40 years.

There is a town in Michigan named Hell. I decided to use this photo of me for this book. I thought it would be inappropriate to smile in hell.

In the early years of my ministry, I got involved with some friends to teach the Book of Revelation. In that study, I developed charts that pulled together specific truths. Some of those charts dealt with the teaching of heaven and hell. One of the charts on hell I called 'Hike Thru Hell.' Another was a comparison of Heaven and Hell. I spent a lot of time contemplating both in that study.

Over the years, I have taught about heaven and hell on various occasions. People were drawn to my message when I preached about hell because it has become a neglected topic in many churches. If we want to honor Truth, we should not shy away from studying and speaking of it just because others are offended by it. We want to honor God.

The topics of heaven and hell are essential because one of those places will be the eternal destination of every human being. Why don't people want to know about the place where they will spend eternity? Ignoring your destination does not change where you will go. Learning about both destinations will help the believer be more concerned about where their lost, unreconciled friends are going and what it will be like where they spend eternity.

James was a youth pastor in Fenton and Lapeer, Michigan. He was then a pastor in Port Huron and Davison, Michigan. He authored several books dealing with spiritual teachings as well as relationship issues. His first wife, Nancy, died of cancer after 43 years of marriage. He is currently married to Lorrie and lives in Lansing, Michigan. They are both devoted to discipling their grandchildren.

Direct comments to
Jolah1968@gmail.com

Please consider writing a review of this book.